ARE WE THERE YET?
ALL ABOUT THE PLANET JUPITER! SPACE FOR KIDS
Children's Aeronautics & Space Book

Jupiter is the fifth
planet from the Sun.

Jupiter is the largest planet in the solar system.

Jupiter is so big that all the other planets in the solar system would fit inside it.

Jupiter is
a gas giant
because it
doesn't have
a solid
surface.

Jupiter has
62 identified
moons.

GANYMEDE
CALLISTO
IO
EUROPA

The largest moon is Ganymede, it is larger than Mercury and Pluto.

When Jupiter
and Earth
are closest
to each other
they are
approximately
391 million
miles apart.

EARTH

JUPITER

The centre
of Jupiter is
a rocky core
and is slightly
bigger than
Earth.

Jupiter is a stormy planet. The most notable is the big red spot which is the largest hurricane in our Solar System.

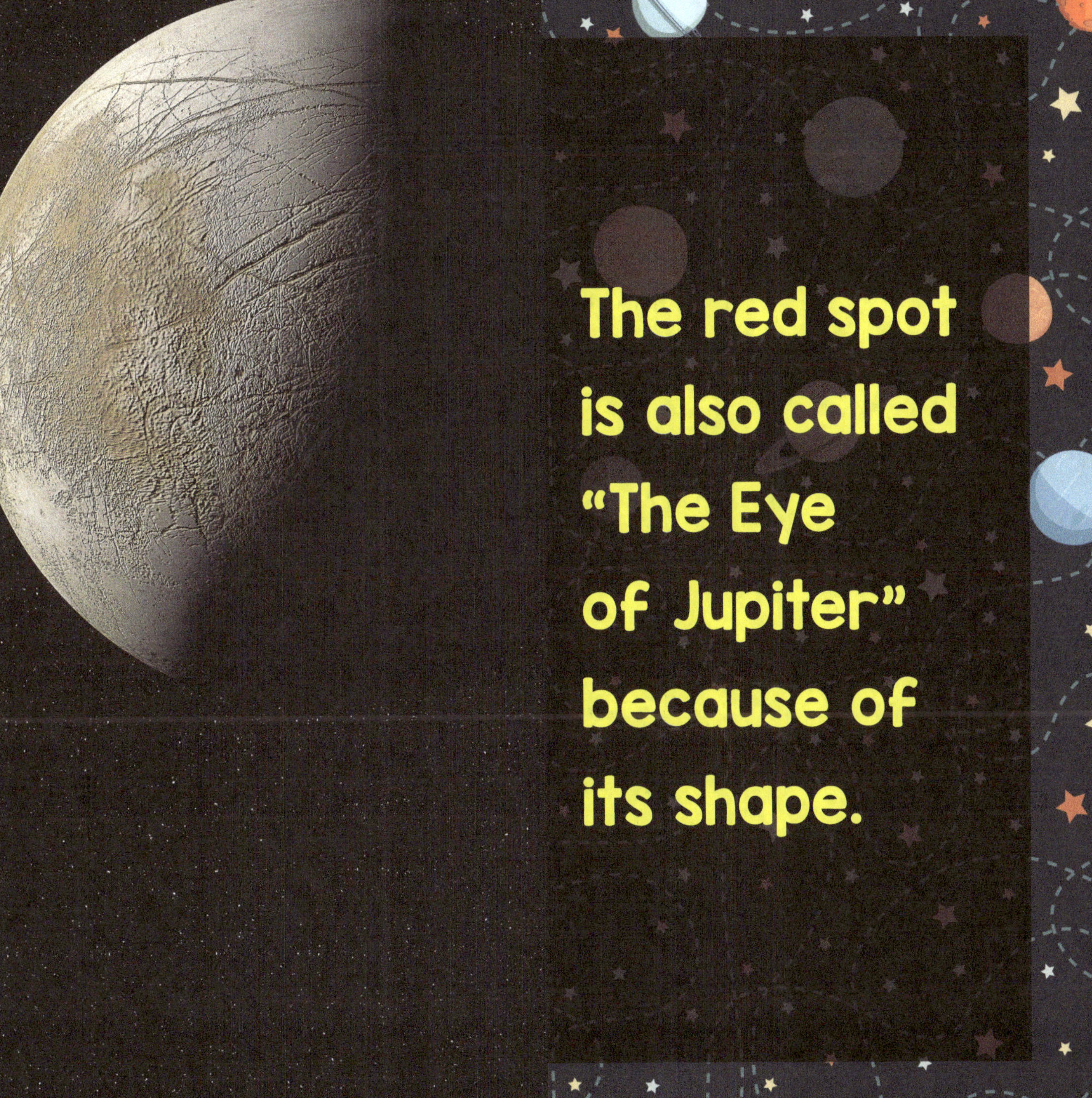

The red spot
is also called
"The Eye
of Jupiter"
because of
its shape.

The distance between Jupiter and the Sun is approximately 466 million miles.

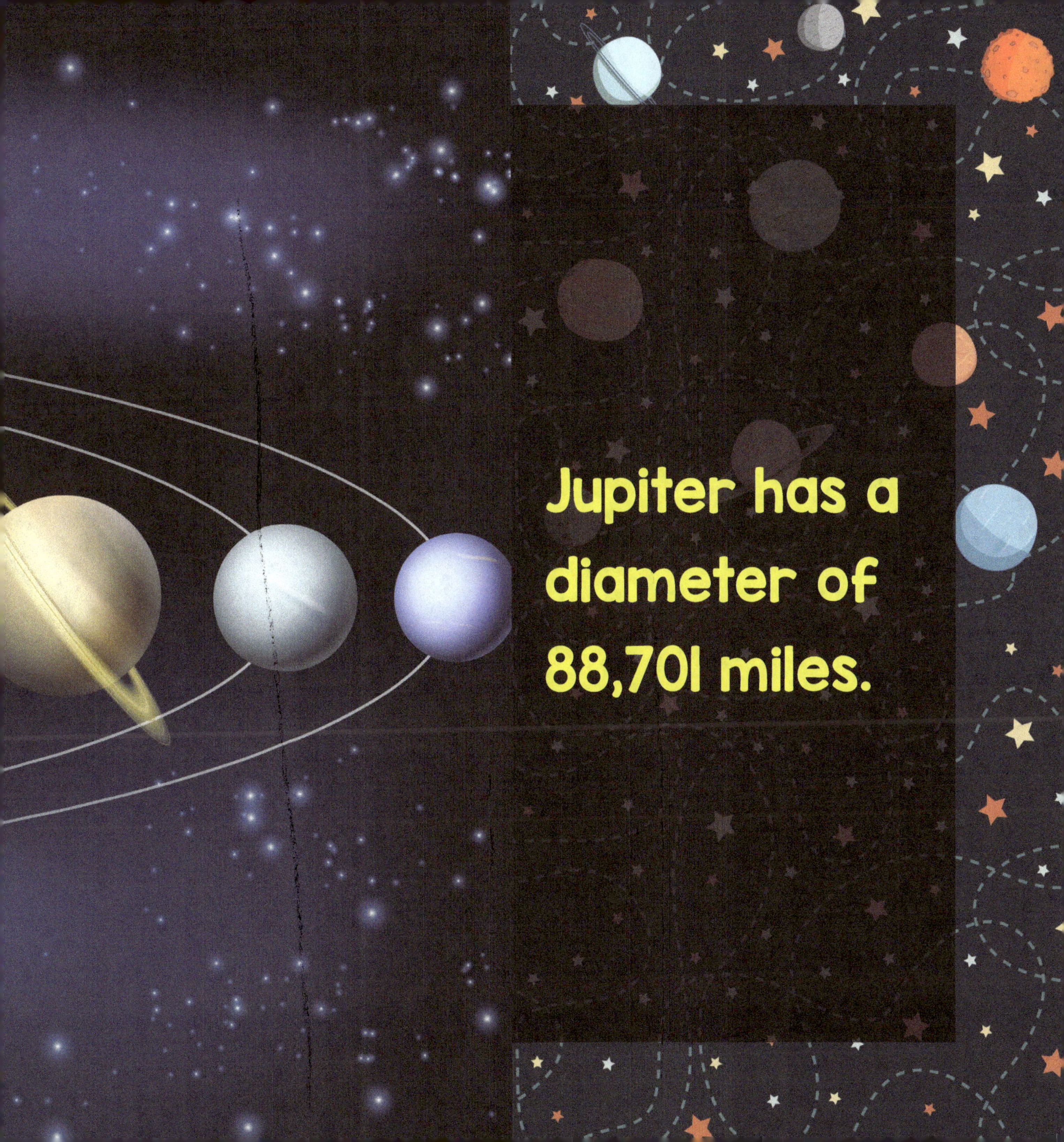

Jupiter has a
diameter of
88,701 miles.

Jupiter spins on its axis once every 9.84 hours. It is the fastest spinning planet in the Solar System.

The first person to discover Jupiter's moons was Galileo Galilei.

Jupiter's temperature is -170 degrees Fahrenheit.

If you weigh 220 pounds on Earth, on Jupiter you would weigh 330 pounds.

Jupiter also has rings similar to that of Saturn but are much less visible.

JUPITER

JUPITER

There are three rings in all and are named Gossamer, Halo and Main.

Surrounding Jupiter's core is a sea of liquid hydrogen.

Our planets are unique in their own special way.

Visit

BABY PROFESSOR
EDUCATION KIDS

www.BabyProfessorBooks.com
to download Free Baby Professor eBooks
and view our catalog of new and exciting
Children's Books

www.ingramcontent.com/pod-product-compliance
Lightning Source LLC
Chambersburg PA
CBHW060619120726
48002CB00010B/3026